FAT,

DUMB,

and UGLY

The

Decline of

the Average American

SIMON & SCHUSTER
Rockefeller Center
1230 Avenue of the Americas
New York, NY 10020

First Simon & Schuster trade paperback edition 2004

Simon & Schuster and colophon are
registered trademarks of Simon & Schuster, Inc.

For information about special discounts for bulk purchases,
please contact Simon & Schuster Special Sales at 1-800-456-6798
or business@simonandschuster.com

DESIGNED BY KATY RIEGEL
ILLUSTRATIONS BY ALAN DINGMAN

Manufactured in the United States of America

1   3   5   7   9   10   8   6   4   2

Library of Congress Cataloging-in-Publication Data
Strupp, Peter.
Fat, dumb & ugly : the decline of the average American / Peter Strupp.
1st Simon & Schuster trade pbk. ed.
          p.   cm.
1. United States—Social conditions—1980—Statistics. 2. United States—Civilization—1970—
Statistics. 3. National characteristics, American—Statistics. 4. Obesity—United States—
Statistics. 5. Consumption (Economics)—United States—Statistics.
I. Title: Fat, dumb, and ugly. II. Title.
HN60 .S87 2004
306'.0973'021—dc22   2003065540
ISBN 0-7432-4945-3

FAT

Percentage of adults in the United States who are overweight: 64.5 (about 127 million)

Number of these who are considered obese: 60 million

Number who are considered severely obese: 9 million

Percentage of Americans considered overweight in 1980: 46

Percentage of overweight adolescent children in 1980: 5

Percentage of overweight adolescent children today: 15

Estimated number of premature deaths caused by obesity annually: 300,000

Rank of obesity, relative to smoking, as a preventable cause of death: second

State with the highest percentage of overweight Americans: Mississippi (26 percent)

State with the lowest percentage of overweight Americans: Colorado (14 percent)

Amount spent by Americans every year trying to lose or control their weight: $30 billion

Percentage increase in the number of Americans to have undergone liposuction from 1992 to 1997: 215

★ ☞ ★

Percentage increase in the number of American men to have undergone liposuction from 1992 to 1999: 385

★ ● ★

Average amount of fat removed in a single liposuction procedure:
1.5 quarts

Fat content equivalent in premium ice cream: 18 pints

★ 9 ★

Gastric bypass surgery procedures in 1992: 16,200

Gastric bypass surgery procedures in 1997: 23,100

Gastric bypass surgery procedures in 2002: 63,100

Daily caloric requirement of the average inactive 180-pound American: 1,800

Calories in one Burger King Double Whopper: 920

★ 11 ★

Percentage by which consumption of red meat and poultry by Americans increased between 1990 and 2000: 21

Average annual meat consumption by Americans: 110 pounds

Average annual meat consumption by Europeans: 55 pounds

Average lifetime ice cream consumption by Americans: 1 ton

Average annual ice cream consumption by Americans: 6 gallons

Weekly ice cream consumption rate, measured in ice cream cones: 3.5

Average annual per capita consumption of sweeteners (sugars, syrups, and honey) by Americans in 1990: 137 pounds

Average annual per capita consumption of sweeteners by Americans in 2000: 160 pounds

Percentage of Americans who believe that diabetes will decrease in the future: 65

Rank of the Baltimore Orioles baseball team among top 50 individual campaign contributors: forty-eighth

Rank of Saban Entertainment (Power Rangers, Transformers, DinoZaurs, Samurai Pizza Cats): forty-fourth

Rank of Slim-Fast: ninth

Percentage by which a croissant at the American franchise Au Bon Pain is bigger than a typical croissant at a Parisian bakery: 100

Average weight gain by a visiting international student during his or her first ten days in the United States: 2 pounds

Total American expenditure on fast food in 1970: $6 billion

Total American expenditure on fast food in 2000: $110 billion

We now spend more on fast food than we do on higher education.

We spend more on fast food than we do on movies, books, magazines, newspapers, videos, and recorded music combined.

Number of hot dogs eaten in 12 minutes at the Nathan's Famous Hot Dog Eating Contest: 50

Number of Quarter Pounders eaten in 10 minutes (heavyweight division): 11

Period for which a 27-inch TV could be powered by the calories consumed in an average American's Thanksgiving Day meal: 49 hours

Percentage by which the volume of a 7-Eleven X-treme Gulp soft drink is bigger than the volume of the human stomach: 50

★ 21 ★

Percentage of public schools in the United States that have signed exclusive "pouring rights" contracts with soft drink companies: 10

Number of book covers distributed to middle schools nationwide with samples of Cadbury Schweppes' Sour Patch Kids: 500,000

Percentage of American children who recognize Ronald McDonald: 96

Calories produced by United States agribusiness daily, per American, in 1970: 3,300

Calories produced by United States agribusiness daily, per American, in 2000: 3,800

Average daily caloric requirement for an adult: 2,800

Average number of Americans killed annually by vending machines falling on them: 13

DUMB

Percentage of voters for whom *Saturday Night Live* and MTV are primary sources of information about presidential candidates: 16

Percentage of voters for whom *Saturday Night Live* and MTV are secondary sources of information about presidential candidates: 35

Percentage by which American expenditures on home video games exceed that of school library materials expenditures: 500

Amount of time the average American parent spends shopping per week: 6 hours

Amount of time the average American parent spends playing with their children per week: 40 minutes

Percentage of Americans who believe that they have never eaten genetically modified food: 70

Percentage chance that an item purchased in an American grocery story is genetically modified: 50

Amount by which the price of a Quarter Pounder with Cheese, small fries, and small Coke exceeds that of a Quarter Pounder Large Value Meal with large fries and large Coke: 25 cents

Percentage of the 10 billion plastic Coke bottles distributed in the United States made of recycled material: 0

Decrease in daily oil consumption in the United States if the average fuel efficiency of all SUVs increased by 3 miles per gallon: 49,000,000 gallons

Rank of the gas mileage among the 35 features Americans say they look for in buying a new car or truck: twentieth

Height of the Ford Excursion: 6 feet 7 inches

Standard American garage door height (pre-1980 residential construction): 6 feet 6 inches

Amount of food suitable for human consumption wasted annually in the United States: 48,000,000 tons

Percentage of U.S. households with at least one television: 99

Percentage of U.S. households with three or more televisions: 66

Percentage of Americans who watch television while eating dinner: 66

Amount of time each day that a television is on in the average American home: 6 hours, 47 minutes

Amount of time the average American child spends watching television, annually: 1,500 hours

Amount of time the average American child spends in school, annually: 900 hours

Amount of time the average American watches television each day: 4 hours

Amount of time the average American watches television each year: 2 months of nonstop TV-watching

Amount of time the average American watches television prior to retirement at age 65: 9 years

Number of videos rented daily in the United States: 6 million

Number of items checked out of public libraries daily in the United States: 3 million

Number of paying subscribers to a Los Angeles–based paging service that alerts customers when a live high-speed car chase is on television: 350

Percentage of Americans who can name the Three Stooges: 59

Percentage of Americans who can name at least three justices on the U.S. Supreme Court: 17

Percentage of Americans who believe that the theory of human evolution is "probably" or "definitely" not true: 47

Percentage of Americans who believe that astrology "probably" or "definitely" is the scientific truth: 48

Percentage of American college students who believe some numbers are lucky: 43

Percentage of Americans who believe we didn't actually go to the moon: 20

Percentage of Americans between the ages of 18 and 24 who can find Iraq on a labeled map or globe: 14

Percentage of Americans between the ages of 18 and 24 who can find Afghanistan on a labeled map or globe: 17

Percentage of Americans between the ages of 18 and 24 who can find the United States on a blank world map: 10

Percentage of 1,500 adult Americans who can name Jean Chrétien as Canada's prime minister: 8

Percentage who gave other answers, including Pierre Trudeau, who died in 2000 and was last in power in 1984: 5

Percentage who said they don't know, or refused to answer: 86

Percentage of Americans in 2000 who said they believe in ghosts: 33

Percentage of Americans in 1978 who said they believe in ghosts: 16

Percentage of Americans who can name even one of the five freedoms guaranteed in the First Amendment to the Constitution: 34

Percentage of Americans who cannot identify the source of the phrase "life, liberty, and the pursuit of happiness": 70

Average number of words in the written vocabulary of a 6- to 14-year-old American child in 1945: 25,000

Average number today: 10,000

Percentage of American parents who believe that their children rather urgently want to spend more time with them: 51

Percentage of American children who say their greatest wish is that their parents would spend more time with them: 11

Percentage of American children who say they wish their parents made more money: 23

Percentage of *Maxim* magazine readers who live with their parents: 22

Percentage of *Men's Health* magazine readers who say they have learned most of what they know about sex from television: 18

Number of children adopted annually in the United States: 120,000

Amount of time it would take the 5 million adoptable children in the United States to find a home, at the present rate: 41 years

Number of Americans who use indoor tanning booths annually:
28 million

Percentage by which the per capita incidence rate for melanoma has
increased in the last 30 years: 100

Change in Americans' daily free time since 1965: +1 hour

Change in percentage of time American parents spend with their children daily since 1965: -40

Amount of free time the average American estimates he or she has per week: 18 hours

Amount of free time the average American actually has per week: 35 hours

Amount of time the average American watches television per week: 14 hours

Amount of time Americans spend on average waiting for Web pages to download daily: 9 minutes

Average annual number of vacation days in Italy: 42

Average annual number of vacation days in France: 37

Average annual number of vacation days in Germany: 35

Average annual number of vacation days in Brazil: 34

Average annual number of vacation days in the United States: 13

Value of annual unused vacation time in America: $19.3 billion

An average American man spent 59 hours kissing a motorboat in order to win it in a contest.

In Wisconsin, if you are *legally blind,* the Department of Natural Resources will issue a variety of permits that allow you to (1) hunt from a stationary vehicle; and (2) hunt with a crossbow.

Percentage of Americans who believe they are in the richest 1 percent of the population: 19

Percentage of American adults who understand that the earth orbits the sun yearly: 48

Percentage of Americans who think that Elvis is alive: 7

Percentage of the American population that has visited Graceland: 8

Percentage of Americans who intend to visit Graceland: 23

Percentage of Americans who believe they have actually spoken with Satan: 5

Percentage of Americans going to college who list making more money as their main reason for doing so: 68

Number of jewelry-related injuries that occur in the United States each week: 800

Percentage of American teens who don't know whom the Revolutionary War was fought against: 20

Percentage of American teens who think the Revolutionary War was fought against France: 14

Percentage of American teens unfamiliar with the term "thirteen colonies": 17

Percentage of Americans between the ages of 18 and 24 who cannot locate either Iraq or Israel on a map: 85

Percentage of Americans between the ages of 18 and 24 who cannot locate Afghanistan on a map: 83

Percentage of Americans between the ages of 18 and 24 who cannot locate the United States on a map: 11

Percentage of Americans between the ages of 18 and 24 who cannot locate the Pacific Ocean on a map: 29

Percentage of Americans between the ages of 18 and 24 who cannot locate Japan on a map: 58

Percentage of Americans between the ages of 18 and 24 who cannot locate France on a map: 65

Percentage of Americans between the ages of 18 and 24 who cannot locate the United Kingdom on a map: 69

Percentage of Americans who would deny an atheist's right to air his views in a public auditorium: 71

Percentage of Americans who would deny anyone denouncing the government the right to air his views in a public auditorium: 60

Percentage of Americans who would deny advocates of "unpopular causes" the right to conduct mass protests: 59

Percentage of Americans in favor of censoring news reports about antiwar protests: 40

Percentage of Americans in favor of censoring news stories critical of the president's conduct of war: 34

Percentage of Americans who do not know that a woman can get pregnant during her menstrual period: 49

Percentage of Americans who couldn't name a single Democratic candidate one year before the 2000 presidential election: 56

Percentage of Americans who could not identify George W. Bush as one of the Republican candidates one year before the 2000 presidential election: 37

Percentage of Americans who did not know who Newt Gingrich was one month after the "Republican Revolution" of 1994: 57

Percentage of Americans on a typical election day who cannot name even one candidate in their own district for any office: 56

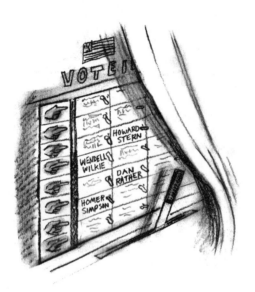

Percentage of American fourth graders who are unaware of the Pilgrims' and Puritans' reason for voyaging to North America: 59

★ 77 ★

Percentage of American fourth graders who cannot name one of the original 13 colonies: 68

Percentage of American eighth graders who cannot recount any of the issues debated at the Constitutional Convention: 90

Percentage of Americans today who do not know whether the Soviet Union was an ally or enemy of the United States in World War II: 51

The most admired American women of 2002:

Hillary Clinton (7 percent)
Laura Bush (6 percent)
Oprah Winfrey (6 percent)
Barbara Bush (3 percent)
Margaret Thatcher (3 percent)
Jennifer Lopez (2 percent)
National Security Adviser Condoleezza Rice (2 percent)

The most admired American woman of 1963:

Jacqueline Kennedy (60 percent)

Number of Americans who use chewing tobacco: 6.8 million

Percentage increase over the last 25 years in the number of Americans who use chewing tobacco: 200

Percentage of Americans who use chewing tobacco who suffer from oral lesions: 75

Amount of chewing tobacco consumed by American children and adolescents annually: 26 million containers

Percentage of Americans who feel that "most people on Wall Street would be willing to break the law if they believed they could make a lot of money and get away with it": 61

Percentage of Americans who feel that "what is good for Wall Street is good for the country": 40

Percentage of Americans who have a firearm in their home: 39

Percentage of Americans who have at least one rifle, one shotgun, and one handgun in their home: 16

★ 85 ★

Number of gun-related deaths in the United States annually: 30,000

Number of gun-related deaths in Canada annually: 1,200

An American's odds of gun-related death: 1 in 9,670

A Canadian's odds of gun-related death: 1 in 26,250

Percentage of Americans who think they will be famous ("well-known, widely recognized") for at least a short period of time: 30

Percentage of Americans who feel that the words "major military power" accurately describe Japan: 71

Average percentage of the world believed by Americans to be English speaking: 52

Percentage of the world's population that is English speaking: 20

Percentage of Americans who expect to go to heaven: 64

Ratio of 18- to 25-year-old Americans declaring bankruptcy to those graduating from college: 1 to 1

Percentage of teens in the United States who report frequently driving automobiles over the speed limit: 77

Percentage of teens in the United States who report not wearing seat belts very often: 39

Average value of a 50-year-old American's assets and savings set aside for retirement: $2,300

Average percentage of disposable income set aside by Americans for savings in 1980: 8.6

Average percentage of disposable income set aside by Americans for savings in 2000: 4.2

Average additional percentage of expenditure by an American consumer if the form of payment is a credit card instead of cash: 23

Number of acts of violence committed in a typical 18-hour broadcast day: 1,846

Average number of murders and attempted murders that a child will witness by the age of 18 if his or her home has premium cable channels or a VCR/DVD player: 72,000

Amount Americans spend annually on Christmas presents:
$194 billion

Percentage of the federal defense budget represented by this amount:
68

UGLY

Average number of pink lawn flamingos sold annually in America: 250,000

The Michigan state legislature voted 53 to 43 *not* to ban tongue-splitting, a "cosmetic" procedure that is also, clearly, a constitutionally protected form of expression.

Percentage of American fourth graders who have been pressured by acquaintances to drink alcohol or use drugs: 25

Percentage of American women who have thrown footwear at a man: 40

Percentage of American women who can belch on command: 42

Percentage of Americans who feel that lack of respect and courtesy should be regarded as a serious national problem: 79

Percentage of Americans who say they frequently see customers treating salespeople badly: 74

Percentage of Americans who have been driven from a retail establishment because of bad service: 46

Percentage of Americans earning more than $75,000 a year who have walked out of a retail establishment because of bad service: 57

Percentage of Americans involved in organized children's sports who have witnessed parents "inappropriately screaming and yelling" at coaches, referees, and players: 71

Percentage of Americans who say they have been subjected to "loud and annoying" cell phone conversations: 49

Percentage of American cell phone users who say they have never used their cell phone in a manner that could be described as "loud and annoying": 83

Percentage of African-Americans annually who are followed around a store by an employee who suspects them of shoplifting: 44

Percentage of Americans who feel that television programs that air during prime time are inappropriate for children: 65

Percentage of Americans who feel that "bad language and adult themes" on television are getting worse every year: 90

Percentage of Americans who would never consider getting rid of TV in their homes: 78

Percentage of Americans earning less than $15,000 a year who report loneliness as a source of ongoing stress in their lives: 32

Percentage of Americans who are very proud to be American citizens: 84

Change in percentage of time that American parents spend with their children in 2000 from 1960: -50

Percentage of Americans who list "spending time with the family or kids" as their favorite leisure-time activity: 12

Percentage by which the risk of a fatal accident increases by having just one teen passenger in a car: 30

Percentage of SUVs among new-vehicle sales in 1986: 2

Percentage of SUVs among new-vehicle sales in 2001: 25

Ratio of space occupied by a typical SUV to that of a traditional passenger automobile: 1.5 to 1

Percentage of SUVs that are ever used off-road: 5

Percentage of the average American's disposable income assigned to personal debt payment in 1985: 62

Percentage of the average American's disposable income assigned to personal debt payment in 2001: 83

Ongoing non-mortgage personal debt level of the average American household: $8,570

Amount of water used in daily showering by an average American family of three: 140–180 gallons

Ratio of teen pregnancies in the United States to teen pregnancies in England: 2 to 1

Ratio of teen pregnancies in the United States to teen pregnancies in Japan: 9 to 1

Percentage of all births in the United States that are to teens: 13

Percentage of all teenage mothers who have a second child within two years of the first: 25

Percentage of eighth grade students in the United States who stay home from school at least once a month because of bullies: 7

Number of credit cards in the United States for every one person: 2

Ratio of total U.S. credit-card debt increase rate to wage increase rate: 2 to 1

Ratio of personal bankruptcies in 2001 to 1986: 4 to 1

Percentage of teenage girls in America who say shopping is their favorite pastime: 98

Average amount of pocket money for an American child, annually: over $230

Average total annual income of the world's 500 million poorest people: less than $230

In America, gambling generates more revenue annually than movies, spectator sports, theme parks, cruise ships, and recorded music combined.

Percentage of Americans who describe "barbecue" as the aroma that best defines America: 39

Number of winter days that the University of Georgia heated its campus by burning chicken fat and other leftover food grease: 21

Percentage of the world's trash produced by the United States:
19

Number of disposable diapers discarded by Americans annually:
20 billion

Number of disposable razors discarded by Americans annually:
2 billion

Number of disposable pens discarded by Americans annually:
1.7 billion

Amount of trash each person in the United States throws away daily: 4.5 pounds

Amount of trash the average American discards in his or her lifetime: 112,420 pounds

Percentage of the world's population living in the United States: 5

Percentage of the world's resources consumed in the United States: 33

Percentage of the world's toxic waste produced in the United States: 33

Daily water consumption of the average American city dweller:
150 gallons

Daily food consumption of the average American city dweller:
3.3 pounds

Daily fossil fuels consumption of the average American city dweller:
15 pounds

Daily sewage production of the average American city dweller:
120 gallons

Daily garbage production of the average American city dweller:
3.4 pounds

Daily pollutant production of the average American city dweller:
1.3 pounds

Americans waste more water in leaks every year than they use taking showers.

Average amount spent by an American on Christmas gifts, annually: $800–$1,000

Average annual income of a Vietnamese citizen: $280–$330

Percentage by which the size of an average American two-car garage exceeds that of an average home in Tokyo: 25

Square-footage ratio of an average American three-car garage in 2001 to the average American home in the 1950s: 1 to 1

Number of plastic bottles discarded by Americans hourly: 2 million

Gallons of oil poured down drains or sent to landfills annually in the United States: 180 million

Percentage by which this exceeds the Exxon Valdez oil spill: 1,600

Ratio of annual energy use by one American to one Ethiopian:
531 to 1

Percentage of human beings who own a car: 8

Percentage of American households with one or more cars: 89

Percentage of the average American's income devoted to car-related expenses: 17

The amount of land the United States blacktops each year is equal to the size of the state of Delaware.

Every single day, 9 square miles of rural land in America is turned over to development.

Rank of greenhouse gas production by Texas among the world's nations: sixth

Rank of greenhouse gas production by France: seventh

Projected average rush-hour speed in Los Angeles in 2025: 15.4 mph

Time spent by an average American watching television commercials during his lifetime: one year

Amount American advertisers spent per child on direct advertising in 1983: $2.68

Amount American advertisers spent per child on direct advertising in 1998: $36.60

Number of advertisements seen by American teens by the time they graduate from high school: 360,000

There are more shopping centers in the United States than there are high schools.

Number of telemarketing calls placed to the average American daily: 2 to 3

Number of the 123 Starbucks outlets in Manhattan that are within 2 blocks of each other: 68

Number of recreational vehicles on American roads in 2002: 9 million

Percentage of American households owning a recreational vehicle: 10

Percentage of Americans who have a tattoo: 12

Percentage of Americans between the ages of 18 and 25 who have a tattoo: 25

Number of bald men in the United States: 40 million

Annual expenditures on hair-growing products containing minoxodil in the United States: $67 million

Annual expenditures on wigs and toupees in the United States: $400 million

Annual expenditures on fraudulent hair-growing elixirs, teas, and horse-hoof ointment in the United States: $100 million

Percentage of American adults who say they are at least "somewhat satisfied" with their physical appearance: 88

Percentage of American adults who say they have undergone cosmetic surgery: 70

Percentage increase in cosmetic surgeries since 1990: 200

Peter Strupp is a middle manager in a Boston office.
He has previously worked as a book publicist in New York,
a theater usher in Chicago, a dishwasher in Indiana, and a snowmobile-
apparel salesman in Wisconsin.